HOW TO RE-IMAGINE THE WORLD

a pocket guide for practical visionaries

Anthony Weston

NEW SOCIETY PUBLISHERS

Cataloging in Publication Data:
A catalog record for this publication is available from the National Library of Canada.

Cover design by Diane McIntosh.
Illustration by Robert Marion and Diane McIntosh

Printed in Canada. First printing July 2007.
Paperback ISBN: 978-0-86571-594-3

Inquiries regarding requests to reprint all or part of *How to Re-imagine the World* should be addressed to New Society Publishers at the address below.

To order directly from the publishers, please call toll-free (North America) 1-800-567-6772, or order online at www.newsociety.com

Any other inquiries can be directed by mail to:

New Society Publishers, P.O. Box 189, Gabriola Island, BC V0R 1X0, Canada (250) 247-9737

New Society Publishers' mission is to publish books that contribute in fundamental ways to building an ecologically sustainable and just society, and to do so with the least possible impact on the environment, in a manner that models this vision. We are committed to doing this not just through education, but through action. We are acting on our commitment to the world's remaining ancient forests by phasing out our paper supply from ancient forests worldwide. This book is one step toward ending global deforestation and climate change. It is printed on acid-free paper that is **100% post-consumer recycled** (100% ancient-forest friendly), processed chlorine free, and printed with vegetable-based, low-VOC inks. Additionally, New Society purchases carbon-offsets based on an annual audit, operating with a carbon-neutral footprint. For further information, or to browse our full list of books and purchase securely, visit our website at: www.newsociety.com

NEW SOCIETY PUBLISHERS   www.newsociety.com

Contents

Real movement begins with vision — with inspiration and engagement, with a pull and not a push.

   Go beyond complaints and resistances and reactions. What truly motivates and inspires is a picture of what the world might be instead.

   Envision changes that are mutually supportive, mutually necessary and mutually in flow. Paint the big picture.

To formulate truly new ideas we need to undertake new styles of generative thinking.

   Nearly anything can provoke new thinking. Watch for suggestive facts: overtones, hints, clues.

   No need to wait; we can actively generate new and unheard-of associations as well.

Certain distinctive tipping points, vectors and dynamics make unexpected openings for creative change-making.

Prepare, both conceptually and on the ground, for the proverbial crises-that-are-also-opportunities.

Systems have immense but unseen capacities for change and self-reorganization — only we may have to offer a certain kind of invitation up front to get things moving.

Behind and beneath the salient social problems lie cultural norms, practices, structures, ultimately even worldviews. These in turn can be shifted and reconstructed. For the most creative leverage we sometimes need to work at the roots.

Some problems virtually follow from the ways in which the world itself is built. Imagine rebuilding!

Other problems are shaped by our prevailing values, assumptions and practices. Here too there can be dramatic room to move.

Worldviews themselves shape our problems — through both practices and structures in turn. Can we re-imagine whole worldviews, then?

Re-entering the struggle with creative momentum, let us rethink where and how we stand and with whom. What are we waiting for?

Optimism, celebration, freedom in expression, cosmopolitanism, good food, good music, imagination itself — since these are our forte, let us start with them to make change.

Got possibilities?

This book is a guide to creative thinking in service of radical social transformation. It is a brief and practical how-to book with examples, offered in the conviction that ordinary people, working together, can begin to re-envision the world in unexpected and dramatically off-the-charts ways.

Please do not say — do not even think of saying — "I'm not creative" or "You can't learn creativity." If creativity can't be learned, then why are creativity experts paid top dollar to teach corporate executives and product designers to be more creative? In fact, why are there creativity experts at all? Why can't the rest of us learn too?

Please also do not think of saying that we can't really change anything, that "changing the world" is only some kind of youthful fantasy. In fact the world is changing radically, right now, right under our feet. Oil is peaking. Genetically modified foods are all over the stores. More people are now overweight, worldwide, than are starving. Earth-like planets are showing up in other solar systems. Tycoons are giving away $30-billion fortunes. Religion is back from the margins, no longer the opiate of the people but more like some kind of intoxicant.

Alternative futures are already on the drawing boards. Corporate CEOs talk about things like "transformational products," and it's not all just hype. Technology magazines like *Popular Science* are beacons of optimism and inventiveness alongside the vitriol and pessimism of the political opinion magazines. The Iraq War alone is now estimated to cost at least two trillion dollars in the end. Quite apart from the advisability of that war, oughtn't we take a moment to marvel at a society that can marshal such an immense investment in *anything*?

Once again, though: what about *us*? Where are you and I, our colleagues and neighborhoods and communities, anyone with some hope for progressive political and economic transformation? Who is insistently talking about what else might be done with even a sliver of that two trillion dollars? Where are the transformational *social* inventions? Who is going to think of them, if not us?

Yes: the first and essential challenge is to think of them. I propose that what we urgently need right now is not the social pressure or the political power to enforce changes we already know we want. That is a recipe for more of the same: more power politics, more zero-sum battles back and forth across all-too-familiar turf. What we desperately need — first — are *ideas:* new big ideas, the next big things, ideas that can reshape or even leapfrog the familiar battles themselves. It's not a time for stock answers or old sectarian battle lines. Our most urgent need is to reawaken the radical imagination.

Case in point: enough of the human race is already on-line that any of us can be in direct contact with ordinary people in Iraq and South Africa and Nunavit and nearly anywhere else in the world. Why abandon the Web to pornography and on-line shopping? We could create a *truly* "new world order", starting right now, out of virtual person-to-person dialogue around the globe. Let web-savvy kids run the forums, translate, instigate: it's their future. Who says that all possible political systems have already been invented?

What about a world with radically less work? What about moving beyond alternative cars, and even beyond alternative forms of transportation, to an alternative *world* in which transportation itself is much less necessary? What about massive new student exchange programs instead of sending so many young people abroad armed and in uniform? What about rebuilding New Orleans as a floating city, or putting only "extreme" surfers in the path of hurricanes? *Now* we're on to something ...

Please don't say (a third request — I know I am asking a lot) that all of this is too audacious, too bold for an age of caution and retreat. For sheer audacity there's not much to top what's happening right now. The Bush Administration's signature projects, just for example: assertively embracing sole superpowerdom; fostering a Western-style democracy in the heart of the Arab world; radically remaking the "business environment." Among other lessons, we need to learn that there is no lack either of boldness or of immense resources in this moment. What we lack are better ideas, a different sense of direction, something quite beyond the all-too-familiar misadventures. It's still the turn of the Millennium, for God's sake, and the question is still what we are going to do with it.

Good energies are already at work. In my own city, a group is working on creating the infrastructure for sustainable agriculture on the county level. Public canning facilities for home gardeners, cow-share programs, Earth festivals. "Re-localize Now!"

A twenty-something former philosophy student is organizing a clearinghouse and open space for forms of learning that don't look like schools at all. A colleague is designing housing for elder visionaries, at once reclaiming a traditional social role and, of all things, re-imagining retirement communities.

Maybe we are beginning to open the door to a freer imagination. Sometimes I think I see it among citizens' groups, in schools and universities, even in politics. Even with the best of intentions, though, it is easy for imaginative work to get thoroughly stuck, and certainly not to get as thoroughly *un*stuck as it might and must. Goodwill and enthusiasm alone do not free us from the usual political and philosophical assumptions — often unconscious. Brainstorms tend to circle back into the usual complaining. The ideas that emerge are often only predictable variations on the familiar. Activists get impatient with all the thinking; they think they already know what is to be done. The doctrinaire mistrust brainstorming on principle: if you already have the answer, what's the point of multiplying options?

So we need help. Creatively and thoroughly re-imagining the world takes specific techniques, shared, known and embraced by all, deliberately and explicitly put to use — even and perhaps especially among activists and the most committed. We need specific ways to make fluid what usually seems to be fixed, better ways to remold it into new and as yet unimagined shapes. You will find them here.

This book does not go into the nitty-gritty of organizing. It offers little strategic advice. It sketches a multitude of examples, but they are mostly forward-looking possibilities not yet actual. The title means what it says: this is a book in service of *vision;* imagination itself in service of changing the world; imagination off the scale, radically suggestive, provocative and fertile. Only a beginning, then — but imagination *is* where it all begins.

Anthony Weston
aw@creativefuturesconspiracies.net
Durham, North Carolina, USA
Spring Equinox, 2007

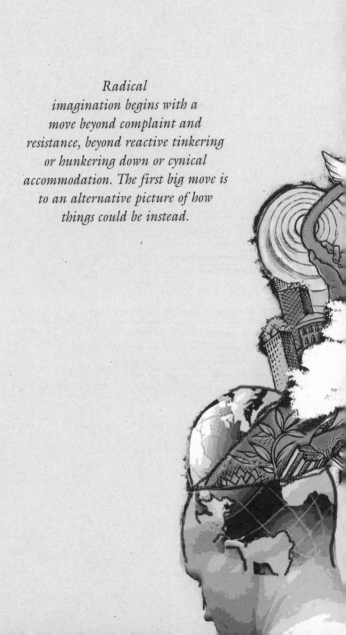

Radical imagination begins with a move beyond complaint and resistance, beyond reactive tinkering or hunkering down or cynical accommodation. The first big move is to an alternative picture of how things could be instead.

1

Work from a vision

Affirmative vision is crucial. Be emphatically, visibly,
clear-headedly *for* something, and something
that is worked out, widely compelling, and
beautiful — not just against the problems or
the powers-that-be of the moment.

Fear and anger push us — yes. But visions *pull*
us, and far more powerfully in the end.

The US Civil Rights movement was one of
the most successful social movements of the last
half-century. Of course it was against things: dis-
crimination, disenfranchisement, the routine
terrorization of whole populations. It took on
deeply entrenched resistance. But it never defined
itself in predominantly negative terms. Always the

language, the imagery, even the demonstrations
and legal briefs and political platforms, were framed
by ideals and hopes. The iconic speech was "I
Have a *Dream*."

It could have been argued — in fact it was
argued all the time by the "realists" — that dream-
ing was a luxury. But who would remember Martin
Luther King's great speech today if he had put all
the same points negatively? "I have a *nightmare*
that the children of former slave-owners and the
children of former slaves will *never* sit down together
at the table of brotherhood … I have a *nightmare*
that my four little children will *never* live in a
nation where they will not be judged by the color
of their skin but by the content of their character
…"? No — it was the affirmative vision that gave
King's words their power.

So where are *our* dreams, today? Cannot we
highlight them just as brightly as our fears —
indeed, like King, *more* brightly?

Take environmentalism. In the popular impres-
sion, environmentalists are the very model of
nay-sayers. Opposed to this, worried sick over that,
ill-disposed by reflex to almost any human impact
on nature. The Voice of Doom. Yet we know very
well what the dreams are. Why are we so hesitant
about them? Speak them out: "We have a dream

that our own children and our children's children will again be able to freely drink the waters of rushing streams, breathe deeply in the morning air and see the glittering stars at night ... We have a dream that we ourselves might be able to come among the other creatures with composure and respect both ways ... We have a dream that the grandchildren of loggers and the grandchildren of tree-huggers will one day work together in a vibrant forest from which they can take what they need without taking its vibrancy ..." This is not just stating the obvious; it is *changing the key*.

Once I was involved in a heated battle to keep a major road from bisecting two state-owned forests — a "connector" to the Department of Transportation, a *dis*connector from the point of view of the other animals and the land. Among other things, the "connector" needed endorsement from the County Commissioners, at that time chaired by a reactionary and fundamentalist insurance salesman universally disdained by progressives and environmentalists. The usual arguments — the road is bad for animals and waterways, it will create worse traffic — went up and just as quickly went down. Clearly it was a lost cause.

In the midst of this wrangling, the head of the anti-road coalition invited the Commissioners to actually walk the route. The Chair, alone among them, accepted. And he returned from that walk, one fine spring morning, persuaded that the road should not be built. "It's too beautiful to put a road there," he declared. The County Commission proceeded to oppose the road, and although it took a few more turns of the wheel to persuade the governor to finally pull the plug, the Commission's vote was a turning point. Why hadn't we highlighted the beauty before — and tied beauty to the other values of intact ecosystems that we had already been speaking for, only too negatively?

Progressives are often cast as anti-business — and sometimes that's what we settle for. Sometimes our economic ideas really are limited to mere rejection. But few progressive critics of business are simply for overthrowing the whole system. What we really want is to rethink, experiment and change. We are *for* more small-scale enterprises; *for* more community oversight; *for* the continuing attempt to harness capitalism's magnificent dynamic energy within a more socially constructive framework. Not just limits on "business as usual," then, and certainly not a pox on the whole capitalist house, but different *directions*. A new kind of "business as usual."

Anti-war? But really *for* multilateralism and the framework of international law. *For* a society that genuinely "supports our troops" by giving them only honorable and truly necessary missions, along with decent health care and family support and educational opportunities back home. *For* giving the desperately necessary "nation-building" tasks following war and other disasters to new kinds of Corps actually equipped to do the job. Likewise *for* a society that honors so many others who also give their daily work and even their lives to build and sustain freedom; consequently *for* a society that is prepared to give them all and their children something genuine in return, like decent education and health care for everyone....

2

Work from a whole vision

Elaborate the vision — paint the whole picture. Frame goals inclusively, mount a campaign across a broad front. Look for overlaps, connections, synergies: ways in which our goals are mutually implicated and mutually reinforcing.

"If you want peace, work for justice." But it's just as true the other way around: if you want justice, work for peace. And to work for either peace *or* justice we have to work for some other things too, like democracy and local self-determination. We seek not a disconnected set of ends, but *another whole world*.

Oppose the current wars or promote local self-determination or environmental protection, but

15

however strong the arguments, you are regularly trumped by a four-letter word: *jobs.* Military production is linked to jobs, whole regional economies depend on air bases or defense plants, and we can't (it's said) put so many people out of work. Military service is itself a job; in fact sometimes it's an essential leg up for down-and-out young people who have no other way. Same for clear-cutting or coal-mining or drift-netting. However destructive some kinds of work may be, people need to eat.

So it is not enough to have a vision of peace or local self-determination or unsullied nature, if these visions are set up in opposition to others, including the usual economic arguments. Change calls for a vision of a workable, peace-based and sustainable *system*, including alternative jobs across a range of sectors.

Since the early 1990s, nearly a hundred military bases in the US have been closed, putting more than 100,000 acres and thousands of buildings up for new uses and redevelopment. Old bases have been turned into everything from malls and office developments to golf courses and environmental sanctuaries. Military industries have tried shifting to other spheres like light rail cars for mass transit. All of this can and must be taken

much farther. Survivalists are buying decommis-
sioned missile silo sites and turning them into
mini-fortresses. How about a few other ideas?
Retreat centers? Monasteries? "Never-Again" muse-
ums? Colleges? Imagine airfields converted to
other uses — new kinds of extreme sports facilities,
maybe, or solar or wind farms. Imagine former
military contractors making musical instruments,
ultra-light planes, mini- or semi-cars, *new* forms
of mass transit or solar units for those reclaimed
airfields. Instead of or alongside the military, capable and dedicated young people (and why just
young people?) might be invited into a vastly re-
invigorated Peace Corps or Reconstruction Corps
for both the USA and the world — with, afterwards back at home, the equivalent of a GI Bill as
well.

You begin to see what a "whole vision" actually looks like: a broad campaign across a variety
of fronts. An organization called the New Apollo
Alliance is now promoting the equivalent of the
20th-century Moon program in the service of 21st-
century national energy independence. Three
million new jobs, they argue, are possible in a
program that *also* serves the environment. Think
solar energy, water purification, biofuels, restoration work, local furniture-building and skilled

woodcraft in place of clear-cutting to ship logs halfway around the world for plywood and pulping. Nature-friendly technologies are often smaller-scale and more decentralized than the familiar kind, which makes for more jobs and more skilled jobs as well. *This* is a way to fuller employment and a vibrant economy, not to mention more fulfilling work. At the same time we are freed from the oil trap, environmentally and politically, nationally and globally; we can turn to seriously rebuilding infrastructure for the 21st century, *and* we may recover a collective, national sense of purpose. A whole vision!

The death penalty is another readily polarized debate. But whether or not a few dozen killers are executed or not makes next to no difference to the understaffed, overcrowded, violent schools for recidivism that prisons have become for *millions* of inmates, not to mention the almost total inattention to victims' needs or to healing the rupture in community caused by crime. Envision instead neighborhoods and workplaces where people really watch out for each other; economies that offer ambitious or desperate young people better work than drug-peddling or petty theft; schools that really prepare youth for such work; a restorative approach to justice that attends to everyone's loss when crime does occur. This is a larger vision that a great many of us can share, even across the usual political divides.

Abortion? Passionate defenders of "life" would hardly rest content if *Roe v. Wade* were merely overturned. There are a host of other things to do: strengthen the family, enhance prenatal and postnatal care, speak to the hyper-sexualization of everything teenaged. The vision here is very big. Likewise, passionate defenders of abortion rights would hardly rest content if *Roe* were secured. Once again there are a host of other things to do, such as, well, strengthening the family, enabling adequate prenatal and postnatal care and speaking to the hyper-sexualization of everything teenaged, as well as equal access to childcare, family leave policies and rethinking the relations between the sexes in general.

Disagreements remain, of course, even fundamental ones, but the "big pictures" are not pure and simple opposites. Whole visions complexify, overlap, draw us back into connection and interdependence, make it possible to go forward *together*.

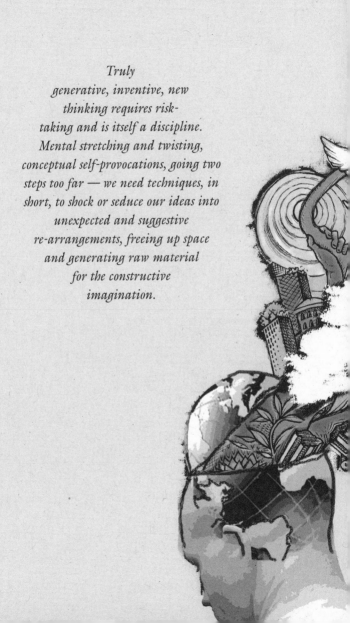

*Truly
generative, inventive, new
thinking requires risk-
taking and is itself a discipline.
Mental stretching and twisting,
conceptual self-provocations, going two
steps too far — we need techniques, in
short, to shock or seduce our ideas into
unexpected and suggestive
re-arrangements, freeing up space
and generating raw material
for the constructive
imagination.*

3

Seeds

Anything we encounter can stimulate new
thinking. Be open to new suggestions from
whatever source. Pick them up and run
with them. Keep running.

ook around. Listen carefully. Listen playfully.
Try out whatever ideas come along, however
unpromising they might seem at first glance. Take
your unfolding experience as a storehouse of suggestions and hints, first seeds of alternative visions.

I am sitting with a group of activists and planners along with some Louisiana residents and
expatriates, re-imagining life in New Orleans and
on the Gulf Coast after Hurricane Katrina. We
begin with the stories: loss, pain, disorientation,

anger. Terms like "recovery" and "restoration" are in the air. We want to affirm and not question people's lives and hopes. Yet at the same time re-imagination is our mandate. Is a new New Orleans possible? A new kind of city, even?

One person laments the loss of her little colony of off-season artist-renters on a coastal island. After they fled, a 30-foot storm surge took out everything. We sympathize. But we also let the story percolate. Artist colonies are expressive, experimental, and *nomadic* ... hmm ... so, what if the returnees consciously and methodically lived as nomads? What if they went back as long-term temporary residents? Why couldn't this sort of neo-nomadism be enabled and enriched — legally, economically, artistically, architecturally? How much would it take?

Dwellings could themselves be nomadic, I am thinking. Indigenous nomads developed all kinds of readily-moved or collapsible structures. Elaborate tents? What would it take to build homes that you could just fold back out after the storm? How about homes that allow the winds and waters to pass through: first floors that are essentially screened porches, maybe, allowing rising waters just to flow under the enclosed second level? How about nomadic utilities as well: portable solar power units, cell-phone networks with a few storm-proof (or floating, or collapsible, or kite-mounted) towers?

Someone else mentions houseboats. The seed of another brainstorm. What about a whole floating city, a city that *embraces* the waters? People could fish for crawfish off their decks. Add the charms of Venice to a re-imagined New Orleans. Aren't there possibilities here? Cities like we've never seen before?

We talk about holidays. Mardi Gras, the spring after Katrina, was half a year to the day from the disaster. Just a weird coincidence, maybe; after all, the date of Mardi Gras varies widely, tied as it is to Easter. And yet, come to think of it (which is what we are doing here, isn't it: helping ourselves to come to think of things), a lot of significant holidays come in half-year pairs. May Day, the holiday of fertility and life ascending, exactly opposite Halloween and the Day of the Dead. So maybe the half-year point from destruction, halfway round the circle of the year, is exactly when we should be celebrating New Orleans and recommitting ourselves to its recovery. Moves are already afoot to make Mardi Gras a national holiday in just this spirit. Meantime some of my friends already take donations at their own Mardi Gras parties and send the money to help rebuild the city. We may have the seeds of a new holiday right here.

To follow out the same logic, "Katrina Day" — the opposite of Mardi Gras, the anniversary of the hurricane's landfall — must also be a festival. But what kind of festival could it be? How about planting sea-grass in threatened dunes and wetlands that buffered the city from storm surges in the past but have been steadily eaten away by river re-engineering? Imagine a holiday season in which all the revelry is out on the dunes, daylong planting marathons followed by sea-grass bonfires and a carnival on the very edges of the sea. And perhaps this too is a kind of Lent, a season of repentance and repair, except this time ecologically.

4

Sparks

Provoke new ideas by deliberately creating
unexpected and new associations of their parts.
Sometimes we need to force things!

Imagination can also get more methodical.
Beyond "seeds" are "sparks" — something a
bit edgier.

Creativity experts give pride of place to what
problem-solving guru Edward DeBono calls the
"random word method," or what I call *inviting
exotic associations*.

The method is simple. Start with a random
"prompt" and then ask what new ideas or associations it provokes when put together with your
problem or question. The randomness, odd as it may

seem, is crucial: that is what immediately gives us a completely novel and unexpected set of associations.

The prompt itself can come from literally anywhere: walking down the street; chance words in a conversation, a film, a dictionary, a textbook, a mystery, a dream. Best is a source with a varied and rich vocabulary — a classic novel, maybe — but in a pinch you can even take words from billboards along the freeway, or turn on talk radio for two seconds as I sometimes do if I am thinking this way while driving. When writing, sometimes even an accidental misspelling suggests a new idea or a more vivid turn of phrase.

Thinking about life in hurricane zones, if I go more or less at random to my dictionary, I come up with ...

"Stir-fry"... this evokes a vignette from one of my New Orleans friends: expatriate Vietnamese fisherpeople who now live in the bayous and grow rice in flooded fields, harvesting shrimp along the way. Once again a reminder that there are ways to live and even prosper right on the edge of the rising sea. How could we seriously facilitate such ways of life?

"Hermit"... first I think of religious hermits ... from there, of the religious dimensions of great storms. Remember that in the Book of Job, God himself speaks "out of the whirlwind" — indeed, archetypally, God *is* the whirlwind. To hear the voice of God, then — who might head *into* the eye of the storm at the very moment that everyone else is headed the other way? God-intoxicated hermits? Other avatars of the Great Mysterious? Why not? And once again: how can we facilitate such quests? Special sorts of hurricane shelters? Lashings to masts?

Devise random or totally improbable analogies or combinations of apparently unrelated ideas, then stand back to see what sparks. And no pre-editing! Thinking about homelessness, maybe, we could try combination or analogy with, say, *sports*. Any ideas? Could homelessness *be* a sport? Crazy, even offensive ... but ... what about homeless people *playing* sports? It turns out that there is an annual World Cup tournament with national soccer teams made up entirely of homeless people — some fifty-odd countries represented in 2006, with foundation support and serious effort to parlay athletic devotion into a route beyond homelessness. How did they ever think of *that*?

Watch for the odd fact, even completely out of context. It turns out that air conditioning is necessary in cars mainly because roads heat up so much in the summer sun. How unfortunate, we

might say. How badly planned! Reframe such little facts as suggestive, however, and you could be
off and running. Couldn't we make roads that are
less heat-absorbent? Why not use less absorbent
materials, or paint the roads white to make them
more reflective (and more visible at night)? Or
couldn't we figure out something else to do with
the heat besides just letting it radiate back into
cars? Install pipes in the roads and pipe through
water to warm it up for home heating or wash
water? Or generate electricity — why not literally
make roads into power plants?

In the end, anything can be suggestive if you
approach it in the right spirit. Cruising the on-
line Museum of Hoaxes one April Fool's Eve, I
found such lovely spoof sites as the Arm the
Homeless movement and the Veterans of Future
Wars. Tasteless, maybe, but there's some sugges-
tiveness here too. Though a spoof of the "real"
VFW, the "other" VFW had 50,000 actual members in the 1930s and was a serious attempt to
provoke people to rethink war through a very
edgy kind of humor — putting children into the
streets, which was bad enough, to ask for their
veteran's benefits *before* their service, because afterwards they'd be dead. Well then ... where might
we go with this now?

5

Stretches

When you want big ideas and big new steps,
deliberately take them. Push beyond incremental
changes to qualitative shifts. Extrapolate and
exaggerate. Make mountains of molehills. When
processes or trends seem to be inching along,
imagine instead going miles.

Sometimes the whole sum of our hopes is a few
small improvements here and there. Raise the
dikes in New Orleans a few feet. Add a few miles
per gallon to the efficiency of new cars. Trim the
workweek an hour or two. But now we are asked
to radically widen our imaginative horizons. Look
for *big* steps: think dramatically farther down the
road, off the scale, out of the box.

Forget inching up the efficiency of cars — why not make them five or even ten *times* as efficient? You can already buy adaptations of the Toyota Prius that get over 200 miles per gallon (yup, that's *200* — though you do have to plug them in at night). How much farther could we go?

Don't ask how to trim the workweek by just an hour or two. Go an order of magnitude farther. Why not cut it by *half*? Economist Juliet Schor points out that since American productivity per worker has roughly doubled since the 1950s, we could have used the gains to halve the workweek rather than increase income.[1] And productivity is still increasing.

Ideas, in short, can *stretch*. Take a deep breath and sit up straight. This is not for the faint of heart.

Last year some of my students took on the task of rethinking the question of traffic around our small but car-intensive campus. One very sensible suggestion was to physically remake the campus to make biking and walking easier and driving tougher. Narrow the roads in favor of bike paths; put in sidewalks where presently there are few; maybe ban first- and second-year students from having cars.

These are good ideas. Each can be worked out and would make a fine contribution. Yet they have at least one foot still "in the box," wouldn't you say? They're a little too predictable. Good, I said, but now *stretch*. Exaggerate. Instead of just creating a few more bike paths and slightly narrower roads, for one thing, what if we took out the roads entirely? Turn the roads *into* bike paths and walkways. Instead of merely creating some non-car options, let's make them attractive, compelling, *wonderful*. Don't just build bike paths, then — put them on skyways, along rushing streams, paint them in neon, light them with sparklers, make them Yellow Brick Roads. And let's not just put in sidewalks, but create sidewalk food stalls, dance festivals, open-air matchmakers and tutoring services.

Massive demonstrations against the US invasion of Iraq were organized around the world by Internet in the space of a week. The result was the largest mass action in the history of the planet. This already is an amazing and suggestive fact. But suppose it were only the beginning? How much farther could we extrapolate? What if we now used the Internet to build ongoing worldwide political organizations based on direct contact between people, and thus ultimately create an alternative to the UN (which is, after all, a union of *nations*) as well as to the nation-state itself? Suppose we even built a whole new representative structure out of this — with representatives' "districts" being virtual, say, including people already in contact with each other all over the globe, rather than geographical? And just by the way: if state and land don't have to be geographically distinct, couldn't we also begin to visualize a totally new approach to ongoing struggles between two peoples claiming the same land?

Gamer friends of mine extrapolate a world government from, believe it or not, global on-line gaming communities. Suppose the original game were itself in some way political, they say — a form maybe of "Civilization." Why couldn't such a gaming community morph into an actual state? A smashing plot for a novel, for one thing, but couldn't it also be more? States have arisen from stranger roots: merchants' associations, beer-hall conspiracies, religious sects, trade unions. Students around the US and many other parts of the world already take part in Model UN simulations. What would it take for a global Model UN to actually *become* a UN: that is, become more than a "simulation"? How big a step would it really be?

Doctors without Borders bring not just medicine but also moral succor or at least visibility to oppressed communities around the world. Great, but why stop there? Already there are Students without Borders, linking students around the world to promote travel, cross-cultural understanding and academic freedom. Now how about, say, Electricians without Borders, or Librarians without Borders, or Musicians without Borders, or Democrats without Borders, or even Philosophers without Borders? How about Weapons Inspectors without Borders? (Now *that* would be something, eh? Work it out: for one thing, there would be no "stigma" to inspections — one of the usual objections — if inspectors went *every*where.) How about Election Monitors without Borders? (This is already happening: think of the post-Presidential career of Jimmy Carter.) And — Elders without Borders?

6

Twists

Thinking "in the box" has a usual, preferred or
expected direction, pre-organized elements.
For creative provocation, methodically reverse
them. Flip the expected directions, think
opposites, transpose the constituent ideas.

Some creative methods play a rougher game.
They challenge us to systematically reverse or
transpose our ideas, turning our usual ways of
thinking onto their heads.

An expected way to improve things is by speeding them up. A reversal, then, would be to think
about how to usefully *slow things down*. Eating,
for example. The Slow Food movement already
claims 80,000 members in 100 countries, devoted

to biodiversity issues, new types of food-growing and recovering the sheer pleasures of eating.

"Slow travel" may be next: there are surely some fine business opportunities here. "Slow cities" and even "slow investment" movements are spinning off in turn. And how about "slow learning": schools of lifelong learning, maybe, that make a point not of how fast they can teach you something, but how thoroughly?

The familiar system is for people to elect politicians. We know the problems: deadwood, too-safe districts, campaign finance abuse, and above all, large numbers of people not really represented by their "representatives." So try reversing it. Initially, you get just a crude thought, a seed: suppose that *politicians* elected *people* instead. But work it out. What could this mean? Maybe would-be representatives would have to go out and try to find a requisite number of people to sign on as constituents. Wouldn't that make an interesting system? Just for one thing, it immediately and elegantly guarantees that our "representatives" will actually represent us — that is, share and advance our views. And the average voter, knowing that they do indeed have a real choice and were actively solicited to sign on, might be much more involved in politics.

Fixed associations dominate our thinking. "Pre-emptive war," for example. Here it is useful to forcibly transpose ideas. What would — just imagine — pre-emptive *peace* look like? Peaceful forms of vigorous engagement way before things become problematic. Cross-cultural poetry forums, maybe. Medical missionaries. Worldwide greenhouse-gas mitigation projects, like massive reforestation or solar installations. Free on-line college courses for anyone anywhere (what MIT, which is already offering them, calls "intellectual philanthropy"[2]). How about a Department of Peace on the federal level and a Peace Academy on the model of West Point, training cadets in the cutting-edge, strategic use of nonviolence?

Think opposites. What is the opposite of cigarettes? Something that could also be sold in packs in convenience stores, I guess, but that is actually *good* to inhale, maybe also something that gives you a little hit of healthy stimulant. Oxygen sticks, maybe? There's probably a patentable product here.

Ready, then? Try this one: what is the opposite of a terrorist? (OK, take a deep breath ... we don't have much creative space on this one yet ... but try it ...)

A first point is that the opposite of a terrorist is not necessarily just a law-abiding citizen. That's merely the absence of terror, the middle point on the scale. I think the answer is more suggestive. The *opposite* of a terrorist might be someone who is an ever-present disruptive possibility, like the threat of terror, except in the other direction. And what would *that* look like? Maybe a person who daily conspires to shower others with unexpected joy. In his book *Pronoia*, Rob Brezsny suggests the term "rapturist" for this role,[3] which I like a lot except that the language of "rapture" is already taken, for better or worse, by certain Christian apocalyptics. A "delightist," then?

What would "delightism" actually look like in practice? Roving bands of youths, maybe, who transform people's yards while they're out. Or paint magnificent murals on freeway underpasses or building sides, or leave flowers on whole neighborhoods' doorsteps, or stage unplanned Shakespeare performances or grand opera or bluegrass concerts or poetry slams in kindergartens or city buses or Wal-Marts, vanishing away afterwards as quickly as they come. Anonymous companies or congregations that give away subway tokens, or food or art, "targeting" the weakest and the most vulnerable.

Put it another way: is a world "free from terrorism" *enough*? Why aim so low? Since the terror issue so often gets framed in religious terms, couldn't we even argue for a religious obligation to spread around radical joy, while remaining, like the terrorist, out of sight and unpredictable?

And if a delightist is the opposite of a terror-ist, what would be the opposite of a *suicidal* terrorist? (A koan for you ...)

7

"The problem is the solution"

Any problem is a complex state of affairs
that, however undesirable in certain terms,
also creates new opportunities. Each new
emergent issue or problem highlights resources
and opens up possibilities that were not on
the board before.

"The problem *is* the solution" is permaculturist Bill Mollison's phrase.[4] It's a good ecological principle — and a lot more.

Power plants produce, among other things, heat. Big plants have huge cooling towers and/or locate where they can discharge large volumes of hot water. The heat, in short, is considered a problem — a waste. And so it becomes.

But doesn't heat have uses? Why "waste" it? We could instead pipe the hot water or steam into homes for heat. This is already done in Scandinavia, where they speak of "co-generation:" the power plant is actually a heating plant as well. When we frame the excess heat only as an inconvenience and a burden, all we can imagine is dumping it as cheaply as possible into the environment. Viewed ecologically, the heat is part of an ongoing process and a potential *resource*.

Don't "resources" of this sort actually lie all around us? As workplace technologies replace more jobs, don't we have an opportunity to reduce the workweek? Why must we cut more jobs while overloading those workers who remain? Or again: shouldn't the threat of terrorism, unwelcome as it is, also spur us to build local resilience: mutual reliance among neighbors for power, food, water?

Bo Lozoff was living in a yoga ashram (a secluded and intensive religious community) when he noticed, with a certain shock, that his life was not that different from the life of a prisoner. Both are very highly constrained and lack many worldly comforts. But his life was *liberating*. So he co-developed what he called the Prison-Ashram Project to enable prisoners to treat their prisons as ashrams. Yes — to make use of the very isolation and "deprivation" and silence that can make prison so awful as, instead, occasions for spiritual growth.[5]

I thought of Lozoff's work when I read recently that Palestinian militants in Israeli jails are emerging as major voices moderating the radicalism of the Hamas-led Palestinian government. They themselves were just as radical before being arrested. "Jail gave us time to think," they say. A spark? What might come of re-conceptualizing prisons as, well, mandatory retreat centers?

Aging conjures up our deepest fears of decline, dependence, death. Still, surely there are possibilities, resources, *opportunities* even in aging — opportunities that we could make more of if we acknowledged and embraced them straight on. There are all manner of specific community needs that older people — skilled, experienced, patient, and (let us hope) freed from the need to continue making a wage — are in especially good positions to meet. Sustaining historical memory, for one. What about systematically bringing older people into childcare? Into the schools? Remember the ancient pattern: in most traditional societies, it is the oldest generation that brings up the young, who induct the new generation into the culture. From the most ancient times, the elders were the ones who advised, mediated, fought for what was right. Now we have the Raging Grannies, embracing their age, who clog the recruiters' lines to keep their grandchildren and everyone's grandchildren from going to Iraq. Doris Haddock, "Granny D," trekked all the way across the USA on her own at age 90 for campaign finance reform, getting herself arrested at the Capitol when she arrived, the people's emissary.

From my friend Bolton Anthony, freelance change-catalyst extraordinaire, I have learned to take the next step: to remember that in traditional societies the older generations are also the natural custodians not just of the past but also of the *future*. Freed from the immediate pressures of survival, reproduction and work, having lived long enough to glimpse the grander flow of time, older people can take a longer view of things. Maybe a little forgetfulness also helps. They are the ones, freed up precisely by the changes that age brings, who can become society's greatest visionaries! Thus the very work this book invites us to — re-imagining the world — might in fact be a prime work of our elders.

Anthony is already hard at work creating councils of elders who take radical imagination as their project, indeed their responsibility. He's adding a new vision of retirement communities as well — as natural homes for such councils. A core group of elders would live in such places and regularly host wider groups, of all ages, for facilitated visioning. Elder communities as creative incubators of the future — now there's a vision for us!

8

What's the next step?

Sustained creative rethinking takes many steps.
Don't stop with the first; keep pushing to the next.
Build on your breakthroughs. If things slow down,
interject new associations. Keep nudging
and provoking ideas to expand,
recombine, reassociate.

The single greatest contributor to sustained
creativity — after a few methods, anyway —
is *persistence*. Or, to put it the other way around:
the single greatest blockage is stopping too soon,
being too easily satisfied with the first halfway creative idea that comes along. It is too tempting to
come up with one or two good ideas and then
consider yourself done. Keep going! Always you

can ask, and ask again, and ask *again:* what's the next step? Figure that you have always only begun.

Along the highway is a huge American flag, flown by a car dealership, always blowing in the wind. I drive along and think: now there's a good advertisement for wind power! It's no small thing to keep such a banner aloft and rippling full time.

An idle thought, maybe, so far. But suppose we take it as a first spark for some serious creative thinking. How far could we go? What it would take to actually generate electricity from a flying flag? These are *big* flags after all; there is a lot of energy there. Someone could make a research project out of this. If we want electricity, though, we might as well use windmills, since they're made to convert wind to electrical or mechanical energy. So suppose these car dealers and other big flag-flyers generated their power using windmills instead? Imagine what driving the highways might feel like then. Suppose such windmills even became a cachet for such roadside businesses, like the flag can be now.

Keep at it ... what's the next step? Of course part of these businesses' desire is to fly the actual Stars and Stripes. Patriotism is part of the cachet. Still, arguably, it's a lot more patriotic to actually *do* something to reduce our dependence on foreign oil and on power plants that damage America's precious lands and waters and air. Suppose, then, that these businesses *also* flew the flag — except painted on their windmills. Then they'd have a very visible way of both displaying Americanism *and* making a clear commitment to environmental sustainability and energy independence — not to mention saving money on power.

In fact, while we're at it, why not plaster the Stars and Stripes on *all* the new energy technologies — hybrid cars, solar panels, even composters? We call them "green," but we could just as easily call them red, white, and blue. There's a whole image-recasting project here, and a vital one too.

What's next? Car dealerships switching to star-spangled windmills ... hmm ... why not *all* corporations? Whole Foods, for one, now buys enough wind-power credits to cover all of its electricity use — in stores, bakeries, distribution centers, corporate offices, everywhere.

What's next? Windmills remind me of the farms back in the southern Wisconsin countryside where I grew up, which pulled up water for the cattle without electrical pumps at all. So why not use windmills to pump city water? Municipal water towers are already nice and high, and there's almost always a good breeze up there.

Despite the "green" nature of wind power, though, many communities and even some environmentalists oppose some wind farms because a large field of tall and ultra-modern wind machines can mar the beauty of the land. Fair enough — it can. We might try to find less visible locations or compromise and install fewer windmills. But why don't we ask how we could create more *beautiful* windmills? Dutch windmills don't strike people as eyesores; they augment and beautify the landscape. New designs are bringing back sails, devising "micro-windmills" for small-scale use, even redesigning the skins of buildings themselves to harness the winds.

What's next? As wind power grows, power companies are renting land from farmers to put up their rigs, which helps out farmers trying to stay on the land — plus they get free power. Saving family farms is certainly patriotic — Jeffersonian, small-town, "conservative" in an old and honorable sense. Mightn't we go farther with this? And speaking of honorable work, as the New Apollo Alliance points out, building and installing windmills and solar collectors on the neighborhood level — plus re-insulating and retrofitting buildings, installing small-scale water purification systems and the like — is an ongoing, skilled and high-demand source of jobs. So we're talking not just about star-spangled windmills but about a star-spangled *job program* here. Big investments in clean energy, transportation and efficiency would quickly and visibly have benefits across the board: a cleaner environment, ramped down global warming and good work for large numbers of willing and skilled workers.

Now it's for you: what's *next*?

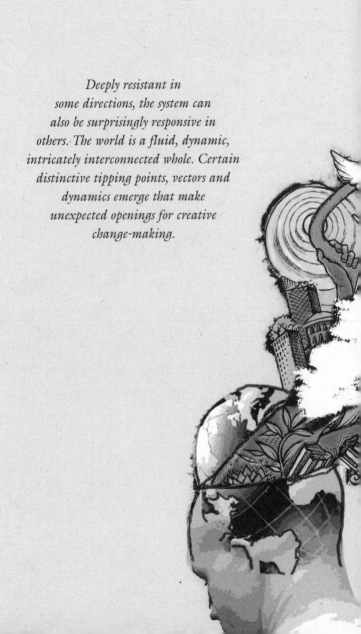

Deeply resistant in some directions, the system can also be surprisingly responsive in others. The world is a fluid, dynamic, intricately interconnected whole. Certain distinctive tipping points, vectors and dynamics emerge that make unexpected openings for creative change-making.

9

Inside tracks

Right now, inside "the system" and even right around the corner, many of the changes we want are already underway. Find ways to join and accelerate change movements already in flow. Radical change is often an inside job.

Naturally we look to the sticking-points, the places where change is most visibly and powerfully resisted. At the same time, though, we may miss the places and ways in which change — complex and radical change — is happening now, already, anyway. What if we joined in?

The oilmen in the White House have consistently blocked US participation in the Kyoto Climate Change Accords. Yes. But the oilmen in the White House are not at all the whole story. Precisely because of their resistance, leadership and momentum have shifted elsewhere — sometimes dramatically.

Hundreds of US cities are already reducing greenhouse-gas emissions to Kyoto standards or better. The Bush Administration claims that embracing Kyoto will harm business, but we already have cities like Portland, Oregon, visibly prospering in part *because* they embrace it. In the absence of federal commitment, American state and city officials joined the Montreal Round of greenhouse-gas negotiations on their own. How lovely to see mayors of medium-sized US cities stepping up to speak for the whole country, a whole new group of leaders emerging! The entire state of California, by itself the twelfth-largest emitter of greenhouse gases in the world, is committed to reducing greenhouse-gas emissions below Kyoto standards — at the co-instigation of its Republican governor, no less.

Nearly all of America's trading partners have embraced Kyoto. Business newspapers already list the US as on-track for Kyoto compliance, because any American products marketed in Kyoto signatory countries must meet Kyoto standards. US automakers selling vehicles in Europe already have to pay for excess greenhouse emissions — which is why Ford and GM are scrambling to offer hybrid vehicles worldwide. One lovely side effect of globalization, don't you think?

Insurance companies have backed action on climate change from the start: global warming is *very* bad for their bottom lines. Worldwide insurance claims for extreme weather events and disasters are already spiking so steeply that the world's re-insurers (yes, there are insurers of insurance companies) are telling their corporate clients to come up with strategies for handling global warming or, ironically enough, lose their own coverage. Meanwhile even the US Department of Defense ranks climate change ahead of terrorism as a long-term threat to national security.

Big Oil itself is on the skids — just think "Peak Oil." Skyrocketing gas costs will quickly accomplish what thirty years of political infighting over fuel-efficiency standards could not: *radically* increase fuel efficiency, and not just in cars but in trucks and refrigerators and factories as well. Again, it's already happening.

Any of us, in fact, right now, can buy emissions permits to cover the pollution caused by our home energy use and vehicles and purchases. For a family of four it's about $50 a month. Under the current emissions trading system, the effect is to preclude the equivalent emissions elsewhere, thus driving up the price, since permits are in limited (ideally decreasing) supply. Each purchase makes it a little more economical for more polluters to invest in pollution reduction than in buying permits. I have friends who give pollution permits away for Christmas — that much more clean air. What better gift?

Still better? Buy "offsets." The principle is: if you are going to emit X tons of CO_2 in a year, you can at least ensure that an equivalent amount is newly sequestered away, for example in mitigation projects such as tree plantings to absorb the CO_2 produced by our cars, or compensated by equivalent power produced by non-polluting sources, such as wind and solar power. In ten years, I bet, massive reforestation "offsets" will be part of the cost of doing business. Whole Foods not only already buys enough wind-power credits to offset all of its electricity use, it also pays less than the market rate for fossil-fuel generated electricity, because its contract is for a ten-year period and was negotiated before the latest price jumps.

I don't mean that we shouldn't also work diligently to bring the federal government along. Of course we should. The point, though, is that there are also other tracks — consummately "inside" tracks — to similar goals. "The system" does not homogenously resist action. To the contrary, there are multiple "inside tracks" to change, right now and right in the belly of the beast.

10

Leverage points

Look for small interventions that can produce
huge changes as the system adjusts. These are
the leverage points: places where manageable
(maybe even tiny) amounts of effort can
have effects across a broad front.
Upstream, small redirections of flow.
Down-stream, everything shifts.

Out-of-the-way structural factors can readily
block or disable change. Some little linchpin
is not in place — by design or default — or, contrari-
wise, is perhaps too firmly in place. Sometimes we
can expend massive amounts of effort and accomplish nothing at all.

Move the linchpin, though, and the system can
shift very rapidly. Thus it is *also* possible to achieve

big things with small efforts. The tiniest adjustment in Federal Communications Commission regulations can make or break media monopolies. Details of food labeling requirements can make or break genetically engineered foods — or organic foods. Real-time gas consumption data in hybrid cars dramatically changes driving habits.

Case in point: with legions of computer-savvy young soldiers now in Iraq, it's no surprise that a huge variety of blogs from the war can now be found on the Web, uncontrolled by either corporate media or the military. Often they include photos and video, uploaded right from the action, seen nowhere else. It's an unprecedented opening, a chance for people of all political stripes to get a gritty, complex, and real-time view of a war half a world away.

Right now the censors are trying to close many of these blogs down entirely, on the grounds that our enemies, all over the Web too, might learn too much from them about military operations, strategy, movements. It's a fair worry. Yet surely there are ways to write the rules that preserve the necessary secrecy without throwing an all-too-convenient veil over everything else. With the smallest push-back — another technological nudge here (digital video only became omnipresent yesterday —

what's next?), a small rule change there (even the existing rules are not being enforced consistently: many pro-war blogs aren't being closed down) — the right to blog might be unassailable. The censors will have to resort to seriously limited rules, and we may for the first time be able to see war unvarnished and unfiltered. Suppose our whole perception of war were to change

Polls consistently show that most Americans would willingly trade periodic raises in salary or wages for periodic reductions in work time. Already we have the second-longest workweek in the world (after Japan) — 46 hours, on average, for those actually employed, while most of Europe has workweeks in the 30s — and the symptoms of overwork are everywhere. Un- and under-employment are high too. Why don't we cut back? Why not redistribute work?

Part of the reason is that we feel compelled to work more in order to afford more intensive activities during our ever-scarcer "leisure" — and more "labor-saving" devices to free up time for, well, more work. We will have to unlearn some deep habits. But part of the reason is also something specific and very simple: right now, for most people, it's impossible to reduce working hours below the normative 40 without "going part-time" and losing most or all of their benefits: health insurance, paid vacations, retirement, the respect and voice accorded to "full-time" workers. Economist Juliet Schor estimates that for the average worker to go half-time reduces his/her overall income by an astonishing 80%.[6]

This is a solvable problem. We need to pro-rate benefits to work hours. Eliminate the disproportionate penalty of scaling back from the increasingly demanding "full time." Schor has a number of other suggestions, such as requiring firms to offer raises in the form of reduced work time as well as increased pay, but simply re-jiggering this one specific blockage might be enough to radically transform work itself. What are we waiting for?

11

Weeds

Promote weedy social change. Aim for changes
(new patterns, practices, institutions) that are as
hardy as possible and that insistently re-emerge on
their own. Self-generative, self-augmenting,
readily drawing on natural desires and
conditions, diffusing widely and wildly.

Too often the changes we seek are like delicate
plants in a garden: they need constant tending,
every year a replanting, constantly pulling up weeds
and worrying about water. Whereas we could seek
changes more like those weeds themselves, the kind
of plant that springs up everywhere the minute the
gardener's back is turned: perennial, hardy, tena-
cious, wily, the kind of plant you can't get rid of.

Unofficial exchange networks are weedy. They spring up wherever you find people and stuff. Friends who live in old-style Midwestern urban neighborhoods of duplexes and alleys report that before trash days everyone cruises the alleys looking for useful items. A kind of running yard sale without the sale. Now web-based auction and exchange networks are multiplying. The Freecycle Network, a pure give-away list, claims 2.5 million members worldwide (it's freecycle.org, *not* freecycle.com, if you look). A running yard sale without the sale — or the yard.

How to expand the reach and transformative power of such exchange networks? What if towns and cities sponsored exchange networks, provided storehouses and helped move the stuff around? What if they were tied in to other forms of self-help and community action? Couldn't we figure out how to "freecycle" goods that are not commodities, like forms of empowerment or political participation or even good cheer? And then it might take only a minor web-ware tweak to begin to build richer kinds of political community on top of such perennial exchange networks.

Co-operative structures are weedy. During the Depression, spontaneous mutualism arose everywhere. A million and a half people joined organizations like the Unemployed Cooperative Relief Organization (UNCRO) and the Unemployed Exchange Association (UXA), exchanging goods and labor without money or hierarchy. Urban agriculture is on the rebound right now (6,000 community gardens in 38 US cities), along with Community-Supported Agriculture (CSA) as small farms link up with networks of consumers looking for good food and a link to the land.

Precisely the sectors where people are most marginalized and excluded are even now generating new networks of self-reliance. Health care, for example: with 46 million Americans entirely uninsured and tens of millions more struggling, health-care co-ops are emerging around the country, including Olympia, Washington; Ithaca, New York; Cape Cod and Philadelphia, where Paul Glover's Philahealthia network offers a range of emergency and other medical and dental services for $100 per year per member and $50 for children. Such semi-self-help networks are not for everyone, of course, but for those in need and with more time than money, they are what "comes up." Once again the creative question is how to enhance and amplify them — spreading the seeds more widely and to other receptive soil.

Sports are weedy. Always games and physical contests entice people, whether on the street corner or at the World Cup (where the 2006 finals were watched by one billion people — that's a sixth or so of the human race). Might it be time to invent some new games? New teams, leagues. Already there are Gay Games, Indigenous Games, Homeless Games. Why not also teams for *causes:* bioregions, endangered species, whole leagues for peace?

Travel is weedy. People get the hankering to move around. How about creating extra-weedy ways to make it easier, such as the exploding web-based "couch surfing" or host networks like Willing Workers on Organic Farms that offer people free ways to live and work and learn all around the world. Hook *this* up, maybe, with Philosophers without Borders or extended youth hostels or visionary communities of elders.

Oh, yeah: and the Web is weedy too.

12

Wild cards

Promote imaginative preparedness. Project
wild-card scenarios and develop "rapid deployment
responses" from new concepts to focused
demonstration projects — ready to go,
conceptually and on the ground.

Every crisis is also an opportunity.

— alleged Chinese proverb

Futurist John Petersen defines a "wild card" as
a low-probability, high-impact event — a surprise that could change everything. There is a
small but greater-than-zero probability that we
will experience a massive plague, or a Chernobyl-
scale industrial accident on the US East Coast, or

an attempted coup or new 9/11s. Quite wonderful or ambiguous wild cards are possible too. Imagine contact with extraterrestrial intelligence. Imagine doubling the possible human lifespan overnight.

We aren't ready. If we orient our thinking only by current givens and probabilities, we will be both conceptually and practically unprepared for radically transformative events that are possible though not so probable. When one does come along, either someone else will take the lead (and don't think for a moment that other interests haven't worked out these scenarios in detail) or else we will all lose the moment floundering around.

Already we are seeing climate-change disasters in slow motion: sustained droughts, monsoons or heat waves in unusual places; disease-bearing insects expanding their range; stronger hurricanes and vanishing glaciers worldwide. Sooner or later, very large and dramatic effects will silence even the skeptics. It will be a pregnant but dangerous moment, a historical tipping point. People will be listening, finally, and desperate for a vision. But we know all too well that disasters can be framed in a reactionary way — as the vengeance of a wrathful God, for example, calling us "back" to something, usually repressive. The wider the scale of the disaster, the louder and more tempting will be such interpretations.

And what will we have to say then? "We told you so"? Maybe, but though the impulse is understandable, it will be worse than useless at that moment. It could readily morph into our own form of repressive blame-assigning. We need to be ready to offer an actual alternative, something less perverse and more inviting, something that looks forward with new vision.

Let us develop new public rituals of acknowledgment and hope: ways to share shock and grief and then turn it together toward reconsideration and reconstruction. And let us, most crucially, have worked-out and workable responses in place. We should be ready to insist not just on reducing greenhouse-gas emissions; not just on "climate-neutral" policies (stabilizing net emissions); not just on "climate-positive" measures like offsetting fossil fuels with solar or wind power; but on *hyper*-positive measures, like reforestation everywhere. Methane fuel cells running on compost. Solar units and micro-windmills ready to go. Demonstration projects already up and running, national models that news crews can film at the drop of a hat. Have an entire alternative infrastructure organized and already in place. The crisis becomes only the invitation to unveil it.

And then, of course: why wait? Let's get going *now*.

Fermenting some alternative theologies might be a good idea too. Environmental disaster as God's vengeance? What sort of God is that? Instead we could picture environmental over-stress more as God's hurt, or Creation's suffering, or a reminder that the Earth has its own profound rhythms and needs — a small turn, again, but it may make all the difference.

Already we get almost daily news of the discovery of new planets. How long before signs of life and intelligence turn up? But then what will it mean to see ourselves as just one intelligence in an unimaginably vast universe? What could it mean to know, in the words of one classic book on the subject, that "we are not alone"? Would our fears overwhelm us? Maybe we'd feel enlarged, to be entering exchange with vastly superior (we assume) civilizations. Or maybe we wouldn't understand a thing and would remain uncertain whether we (or they) were dealing with intelligence at all. Aldous Huxley once declared that extraterrestrial intelligence is likely not only to be stranger than we expect but stranger than we *can* expect. A fair point, considering that we have enough trouble even appreciating each other's intelligence — sometimes even our own.

In any case, shouldn't we work some of this out? For starters we could learn to rejoin and rejoice in the vibrantly intelligent and often "alien" enough world that *already* lies all around us, right here and now.

13

Hidden possibilities

> Everyone and everything have enormous
> capacities for change and self-reorganization.
> The world will respond in the direction of our
> invitations — but we may need to make the
> offering, the invitation or even leap of faith, first.
> Overestimate everything!

Systematically enough oppressed and excluded,
groups considered ineducable — women, slaves,
ex-slaves, the children of the poor and so on —
really were *not* capable of formal learning. Those
doors had to be opened *first*. The same can be said,
much more recently, of women's sports. Title IX
was a fluke (now there's a story), but once in play
it changed everything.

Once in play — yes. It's a tricky business. The possibilities weren't, aren't, visible up front. So the question remains and in fact always will remain: what possibilities do *today's* actualities hide?

What if schools consistently pitched expectations two levels above what students (even teachers) think is possible? Those totally unlikely success stories — the inner-city middle school chess team or martial arts club that takes the national championship, the service project or science fair that changes everything — suppose they are not the exceptions but everyone's capacity all the time?

What if criminals of all sorts came into face-to-face dialogue with their victims and/or families? The stereotypes tell us it could never work. But already there are more than 300 "Victim-Offender Mediation" programs around the US doing just this, coupled with various forms of prison and community ministry. Both sides ask questions, express their feelings, struggle together. Mediators help them arrive at "next steps" — sometimes financial restitution, treatment plans, community service and more creative options too. Internationally, there have been more than 20 "Truth and Reconciliation Commissions" on the model of South Africa, which emerged from apartheid by an enormous leap of

faith, confronting the evil and building reconciliation. Everyone expected a bloodbath. The totally
impossible happened instead.

Neighborhoods or cities that seem passive or
self-preoccupied in the face of even minor threats
can be roused and electrified, united in action, to
support a local basketball team or to clear fallen trees
after a hurricane. Are we really such individualists?
Even the business world requires collaboration
rather than competition within companies in
order to compete effectively outside. Not to mention families, schools, symphony orchestras,
bridge clubs, charities of all sorts, the army and
so on.

So the task is not to make people less selfish.
We're already much less selfish than the stereotypes say, and always have been, though there is a
certain self-fulfilling illogic to the selfishness
stereotypes too. The task is to call more effectively
upon the intense social energies that already run
through our lives. Take artistry for example. Suppose
classroom walls were routinely decorated by student murals? Suppose that people began to break
up the uniformity of highways or office buildings or
hotel rooms with on-the-spot art, like sand sculp-
tures on the beach, but everywhere and more
lasting? What unsuspected expressiveness might

show itself then? Would most people still take a pass? Would you? Really?

Finally: think of factory farms. Animals are deliberately reduced to the most pitiful, stupid, anti-social cripples. It makes the exploitation and the slaughter easier, and the animals don't end up seeming like plausible candidates for rights or any kind of moral consideration at all. Wild animals are reduced to "game," who then naturally play the parts — whales attacking whalers, who after all are trying to kill *them,* or more often running for their lives — while noise, disease and "multiple uses" degrade forests which then hardly seem worth saving.

Here too, recovery may begin with an offering, an invitation. There are now musicians, trying for courtesy for once, who play orca-like arpeggios and ragas through underwater speakers in the middle of Puget Sound, inviting response — and wild orcas may come and jam for hours. On the Web you can buy CDs of these sessions. Whale-watching replaces whale-hunting, sometimes even in the same boats, and we learn that many whales are extraordinarily affectionate. Many now seek out human company. Bioregionalists are committing to long-term care and residency in a single place, and there are now even "eco-steries" on the

model. of medieval monasteries committing themselves to the same care over generations. What
might they discover, after a few hundred years?
There's only one way to find out ...

Beneath the
problems that often seem so
"given" lie cultural norms and
practices and ultimately whole worldviews. Our problems have contexts,
backgrounds, roots. These in turn can be
shifted and reconstructed. Problems
can be circumvented or at least
reshaped so that they arise in
more manageable forms.

Go deep. The word
"radical" itself comes
from the Latin "radix", root.
For the most creative
leverage we sometimes need
to work at the roots.

14

Rebuild from the ground up

When systemic problems are created by the ways
we make or build things — quite literally — our
most creative opportunity is to remake those very
things. Rebuild from the ground up.

The best approach to the challenge of recy-
cling is to eliminate the need for it in the first
place. Redesign products and packaging so that
they never become junk at all. Make products that
compost rapidly or have other attractive uses:
building blocks, collectibles, toys. Promote fast
foods in edible wrappings like tacos and cones so
that there is no waste!

Take the car. We know its problems all too well:
death and mayhem on the roads; air pollution and

global warming; noise everywhere; lifetimes lost to traffic jams and commuting even when the roads are "clear"; dysfunctional cities; military quagmires halfway around the world and industrial adventures despoiling even the pristine Arctic.

We are getting creative with cars, sure. Demand for hybrid cars already vastly exceeds supply. Fuel cells and hydrogen engines are on the horizon, with enormously improved efficiency and no emissions except water. Clever college students spend an afternoon retrofitting their engines and then drive across the country on donated vegetable oil, or "biodiesel" — the exhaust smells like french fries.

None of this, though, will solve the deeper problems of the car. Loss of time, money, land, peace — these will only get worse. It's a structural problem. Ultimately the car itself must go.

There's mass transit — trains, bus systems, bike trails. Planners are already designing high-density developments around new transit stops so that people can walk to shops and work and home from the stops without driving at all. There are already foldable briefcase bikes in the Netherlands; totally coordinated multi-mode public transit systems; legendary bus systems like Curitiba's in Brazil, with the same performance as subways at a tenth of the cost.

This is good work. Yet we are still not at the actual root of the problem. The real problem is that we need, or think we need, to travel so much in the first place. Suppose we took it as a goal not to provide better cars or even, mainly, better non-car transit, but to dramatically reduce the *need* for travel itself. Suppose we build communities where work, school, friends and family and food are available without the need to go any serious distance. Suppose we make shopping local again, with corner groceries and farmers' markets, augmented by Internet shopping for less commonly sought or more durable goods. Create new jobs based at home or from local community tele-centers, combinations of branch libraries with a sort of copy-shop-cum-Internet-café. Plus childcare centers, schools, gardens. Sweden is already building such "tele-cottages" nationwide. Promote "virtual travel," and when we take actual trips, take them long and slow: walk, bike, take a camel.

Notice that many of the pieces of such a post-transport world are here already: the electronic infrastructure; an energetic co-housing movement and history. And even now we are not so far past a pre-transport world. In much of the rest of the world, bicycles are still a form of transportation and not simply recreational equipment. But again:

we need to *build* differently to make their possibilities real.

Another case in point: despite the missed opportunities to raise the dikes and despite all the inept responses after the flooding, the root of the New Orleans disaster is that here is a city well below sea level to which the sea is coming ever nearer. And New Orleans is only the most vulnerable city of many. All up and down the US Southeastern and Gulf coasts we have built fragile buildings and brittle infrastructures — bridges, roads, power lines — in zones periodically swept by high winds and flooded by storm surges, both of which are getting stronger.

People may choose to rebuild in certain places anyway. If so, we must surely also restore all the buffering nature can offer: the thousands of square miles of wetlands that once buffered New Orleans, for instance, destroyed by ill-considered shipping channels and indiscriminate underground pumping.

The key thing, though, is to imagine entirely different ways of inhabiting hurricane-prone areas — to reconstruct coastal life itself in a new key. Maybe few permanent residences, only the most resilient infrastructure, *im*permanent and moveable, coupled with the kinds of presence that actually welcome storms: new kinds of extreme sports, maybe, or "nature music" festivals. Portable solar power units, cell-phone networks. The outermost regions for the campers and fisherfolk, birdwatchers (hurricanes fling in all sorts of uncommon birds) and houseboaters (who can *move*). And couldn't whole cities embrace the winds and the waves? What about a city that floats?

15

Cultures and practices

When systemic problems are created by cultural
norms and practices, our most creative opportunity
is to reshape those practices themselves. Along
with issue-based activism we need a culturally
transformative pro-activism.

It's not only the built world that shapes certain
problems. We may also need to re-imagine our
habits and practices. We would get a long way
toward a sustainable world, for instance, just by
requiring manufacturers to take their products
back at the end of their useful life — as the
European Union already does. *Then* we'd get
reusable parts in a hurry, and ultimately products
made to last.

"Preemptive peace" is a reversal of "preemptive war" — a strategy of heading off conflicts before they threaten to turn lethal, averting them at their roots. Imagine parallels everywhere. Preemptive corporate ethics? It's a lot easier to prevent corporate malfeasance than to clean up or mitigate the wreckage afterwards. A few public representatives on corporate boards of directors could work wonders. How about preemptive religious tolerance? Suppose — to take Garrison Keillor's old joke seriously — we really do need Unitarian missionaries?

How about preemptive *welfare?* The Scandinavian strategy is to prevent people from falling into poverty in the first place rather than grudgingly trying to pull some individuals partway out once they get there. Good health care and decent housing and transportation for everyone. Walkable cities. Serious civic effort to keep good jobs in town. Make a decent life cheap enough that even people with very little money are not disempowered and isolated — the real essence of "poverty" in any society.

We know the toll from drugs — that is, illegal and often ferociously addictive mind-altering substances. We know the toll from the so-called "War on Drugs" too, not to mention that on the whole drugs are winning. No doubt there are certain leverage points. No doubt too there are social innovations that could make some presently-illegal drugs far more benign than alcohol. Amsterdam has a system of bartender-controlled marijuana, for example. Such ideas are worth exploring.

The reconstructive questions, though, are more basic. Why are so many people tempted by drugs in the first place? Where is the deep compulsion? Surely part of the allure is that drugs offer some excitement in the midst of an otherwise uninteresting or maybe utterly discouraging life. Work (or not), school (or not), family (or not), routine, boredom ... no way out. Drugs aren't just an escape; they fill a genuine need that otherwise people may find hard to meet.

Aren't there less lethal ways to make life more interesting? Why don't we create more team challenges of all sorts for all sorts of people — math contests, orienteering, Habitat for Humanity multiplied by ten — where losing your edge is letting down your teammates and you have a ready-made support group for "natural highs"? Think also of recovering the challenge and astonishment of the world as it is: rivers and mountains and sunrises. Kayak the whitewater, camp out in the middle of a midnight thunderstorm. Why isn't *that* part of education, for starters — as it certainly is for indigenous peoples?

Where's the natural *ecstasy,* even? In his book *Wild Hunger,* Bruce Wilshire attributes the allure of drugs partly to "ecstasy deprivation," a new and wild kind of deficit disorder.[7] "Ecstasy" literally means standing outside of yourself. There are religious ecstasies, sexual ecstasies, creative and athletic and scientific ecstasies ... but all of these need recognition and practice. Here, surely, is a worthy and deeply intriguing cultural challenge, and for everyone from fundamentalists (some of whom, in their way, meet it better than the rest of us) to musicians, martial artists, science teachers, Outward Bound instructors, computer programmers, dancers ...

Really, seriously: how can we make life more ecstatic? Why should we perpetuate a culture only concerned with cheap thrills and pass-the-time entertainment? There's a little more to do than that, and it's certainly not just saying NO a little louder. Meanwhile, back at work and school, what if even these everyday and necessary forms of life were actually engaging — almost too much, sometimes, in their intensity? What a life it could be ... and where would drugs be then?

16

Worldviews

Systemic problems trace back in the end to worldviews. But worldviews themselves are in flux and
flow. Our most creative opportunity of all may be
to reshape those worldviews themselves. New
ideas can change everything.

Along with battling pollution we also need to
ask how we ever got into the position of thinking of the natural world as a place to dump it in the
first place. Along with battling poverty we need to
ask why we tolerate radical inequality at all. In many
African tribal societies, even a single homeless person
is felt as a disgrace by all. How did *we* get where we
are? These are philosophical questions — indeed
— and another kind of root at which we can work.

Fundamentalists in huge numbers believe they are living in the Last Days. The Web crackles with arguments about the timetable of "The Rapture" — when the Elect will ascend to Jesus and the rest of us will finally get eternal hellfire — and about who exactly will be saved. Call it escapism (that bumper sticker "Come the Rapture, this car will be driverless"), call it revenge fantasy, call it what you will, but there is immense energy here for a sense of direction, meaning and for change.

Secularists either ignore "rapturism" or engage it only to ridicule it ("Come the Rapture, can I have your car?"). But nothing is offered in its place. It's not enough just to push people back toward private hedonisms and small-scale hopes. Most people will not resign themselves to a universe that offers no hope. Discussing all of this one day, the poet Nancy Corson Carter found herself talking about "Rhapsody" in place of "Rapture." All right then … if they have Rapture, suppose *we* have *Rhapsody:* music, harmony, literally the singing of epics (the original "rhapsode" was a reciter of Homer) — or, more broadly, a beautiful world. A world where beauty is rugged and engaging and persistent, a creature of daily things and of our own hands.

It's said that at first contact the native people of the Americas had an impossible time understanding

Christianity's idea of a paradise somewhere else. Paradise was so obviously *right here*. So how do we have to rethink "this" world to awaken to it as paradise? Shifts of worldview are invited, but they are nothing like shifts merely to the opposite side of the currently polarized "debate" — evolutionism from creationism, agnosticism from fundamentalism. They are shifts away from that entire scale. Supposing that we *already* live in paradise, in rapture — what then?

The modern secular "paradigm" can be nailed down in various ways. It's "Materialism" in the philosophical sense: the belief that the world consists of mostly inanimate matter on the one hand and minds, mostly ours, on the other. Or it's "Mechanism," the view that the world and maybe even minds work according to reductive physical laws. Or it's a purely instrumental and atomized view of nature in which the world exists in disconnected pieces, available for our use, and what goes around mostly just goes away. Even religion enters this picture on Materialism's own terms: the "spiritual" is supposed to stand apart from this world, and indeed must be defended with increasing desperation or dogmatism.

But this modern paradigm itself is on the skids — all of it, and not just in small ways but altogether.

The entire ground is shifting. Maybe, just maybe, the world does *not* reduce to simpler and more manipulable components. People from across the disciplines are beginning to insist that "wholes" matter, that the whole is animated in ways we have as yet only glimpsed by intuition or metaphor and that (re)connecting to this larger flow of things, and soon, is our best hope of flourishing or even surviving. Thus the outlines of a successor world-view are beginning to emerge, and not merely a kind of reflex denial or reversal but another coherent and compelling world-organizing framework. It is, just possibly, a vision of the world as a living web in which *connection* is key, and mutual co-constitution is the way of all things.

Everything must then be viewed differently. Imagine political communities founded on Affirmations of *Inter*dependence rather than Declarations of Independence: bioregional, deeply participatory and decentralized; spontaneous, festive and multiple in their forms. In social organization, nothing so simple as a top-down command structure dispersing "human resources," but a collaborative enterprise, a far more intelligent and responsive structure, calling for totally different models of leadership as well. "Medicine" might now be recovered in the worldwide indigenous sense, as an intervention in the whole human relation to the universe. "Environment" too now plays in a new key: not as a separate, endangered sphere needing better management for "maximum sustainable harvest" but as an essential element of our very identities, the *whole* world and not just the *rest* of it, and a living web itself.

Re-entering the struggle with creative momentum, let us rethink where and how and with whom we stand, how we take up issues, even how we speak. There is space for inventiveness and originality here too, and big moves to be made.

17

Play to your strengths

> Open-endedness, inventiveness, community,
> cosmopolitanism, dialogue, inquiry, sense of
> humor, freedom in expression, good food, good
> music — since these are our forte, let them lead
> our change-making.

I am talking with a young friend, veteran of demonstrations and other actions in the US and Canada and Europe. How do we resist established power, we ask, without turning into its mirror: joyless, self-righteous, exclusive?

She says: we must be the change we wish to see in the world. Make demonstrations into festivals, she says, inventive, celebratory, open-ended. Invite everyone — even the cops, even those against whom the protest is directed.

I say: yes — there's power in changing the game this way. The guardians of order are not prepared to be invited to something else. It's "disarming" in a double sense. Moreover, there is an *argument* here: a case for another world, another way of living. "Being the change you want to see in the world" is itself a way to make change.

Humor, for one thing. Good humor is subversive, irreverent and tends to undercut the powers-that-be. It is no accident that there is no right-wing equivalent of *The Daily Show* or *The Onion,* and that fundamentalists erupt in fury over mere cartoons. All but the most desperate of our demonstrations have their playfulness and their theater, their puppets and masks and dancing. They are not bitter or cynical (we hope), but an insistent reminder that something better and more worthy is possible, that there are always alternatives. The way we see ourselves or the world is not the only way we or it might be seen. At the Montreal Climate Change Convention, youth from all over the world lobbied official delegates with formal visits but with irresistible humor and drama too, staging a funeral for ice hockey, Canada's global-warming-endangered national sport, on a slushy day, and handing out fortune cookies to the delegates with messages like "You will make decisions with your children in mind."

Celebration too is our strength and our passion. It brings together many other values: community, artfulness, pleasure right here and now. Currently you could argue that we have a holiday shortage — certainly by comparison with the people of medieval Europe, supposedly worked to death, who by some reckonings had well over a hundred non-work, festival days — actual holidays, that is, "holy-days" — per year, not merely "vacations" (literally, empty time). We need more!

How about a celebratory environmentalism? Imagine new festivals for animal migrations, hawk- or whale-watching, like the Japanese festival for the return of the fireflies? Planting and harvest celebrations again — and let's grow enough of our own food to have something to celebrate! Lights-Out Nights to watch the moon and the stars and meteor showers and comets — together. We can reclaim the old holidays too: the solstices, the equinoxes, the great cycle of light and dark, of the year and the seasons, New Year's and Christmas the rebirth of the year; Easter and Passover and Vernal Equinox the resurrection of life; May Day halfway around the circle from Halloween, fertility and death in their endless interlocked dance. *This* is how we learn to love the Earth — and we defend what we love.

How about funerals *before* death? We could choose our own funeral times and organize a celebration of a life well lived much as we now celebrate bat mitzvahs or marriages, and then after that, we could live in a different way ... or not.

"Teach the controversy," fundamentalists say. Put Creationism into school curricula, they argue, give it a fair shake and look at challenges to Darwinism. And why not? Really, why not? We academics are good at controversy. Serious, sustained, "reality-based" dialogue, with multiple views in play, is our *specialty*. Think of how the teach-ins made the critical space for the anti-war movement in the Vietnam years; in a small way they are being revived in the face of the Iraq wars. We need to do more of this, not less. Invite everyone, but spare no criticism either.

Let's "teach the controversy" everywhere. Open up multiple issues and promote critical thinking generally. How many creationists favor "teaching the controversy" regarding, say, the War in Iraq or gay marriage or (God forbid) alternative religions? How many of those creationists so sanctimonious about intellectual openness actually teach the same controversy (that is, give *evolution* a fair shake) in their own schools? Do they put "Only a Theory" stickers in their Bibles? But we can't highlight that hypocrisy if we ourselves are dogmatically insisting on Darwinism. And when Creationism claims the stage, where are the Native American stories? Greek mythology? Are they even "teaching the controversy" *within* Creationism? It's there to be taught.

18

Reclaim the language

Reclaim the actual meanings of words, including more inclusive and edgier meanings latent in the terms we are already using. Adopt new terms that match our new thinking, or terms that themselves enable new thinking.

Every word, with its overtones and associations, already gives the world a certain shape. Just as it highlights certain aspects it also pushes others into the shadows. These days we can't even speak of "reality" itself without the adjective "harsh" coming up in the next breath, or maybe the bizarre phrase "reality TV," while the *actual* realities of the times stay out of focus. To see our way to real change, we need to reclaim the language itself.

Maybe we should all declare ourselves **Conservatives** and just be done with it. Then we can debate with our fellow conservatives about what to conserve first. Plenty of options: civil liberties; the fragile beauty of this land; the small towns everywhere being strong-armed by Wal-Mart ...

The Culture of Life — a truly great phrase. Why abandon it to hardliners mostly preoccupied with the most marginal and transitional stages of life, important as those may also be? What about serving "life" as in, say, cleaning up the air and water, or decently feeding the half of the world's children who go to bed hungry every night, or even just remembering that global climate change endangers fetuses too? *We* are for the culture of life — big time. Especially for actual, live, regular people. Don't fight the term: let's persistently and eloquently claim it for our own. And then make it seriously radical.

When did **Social Security** get reduced to a pension? Real security in old age has got to mean more than the money to buy yourself some minimal health care and maybe an occasional housekeeper. It means having a family life and a community in which you have a place and a contribution, and in which others take care of you in turn as a matter of course. That is, it's *social*. The Amish say that their "social security" is their community. If the barn burns down, they don't need insurance payments to hire a contractor to rebuild it. They rebuild it themselves — friends, neighbors, families; colleagues, companions, co-religionists.

And why do we allow **Homeland Security** to be reduced to airport frisking and universal paranoia? What if we actually did think about how to protect and enrich our home land? Even progressives speak fearfully of "attacks on our soil," meaning terrorism at home, forgetting how aggressively "our soil" is under intense attack *already.* Organic farming, watershed and wildland preservation, de-automobilizing cities — *there's* Homeland Security for you! Not to mention the great philosophical secret of the martial arts: that we will only truly be secure when our erstwhile enemies no longer desire to attack us. So what if our primary interventions abroad were medical or educational, musical or ecological or even philosophical? And again: we can frame this project precisely in terms of security as well.

We may rethink even the language of the **War on Terror.** If terrorism is pictured as a crime rather than a military assault, then the natural response is not war but criminal prosecution. Law enforcement, not invasions. If terror is conceived as a nuisance, as John Kerry too timidly proposed in the 2004 US Presidential campaign, then the natural response is something like "management" and crime control. Immediately we are in a very different political space.

Terrorism suggests an ideology, **terrorist** a career. Suppose we thought of it instead as violent desperation — call it "Desperationism," perhaps. By looking more toward the condition of the perpetrator and less toward the intended effect on the victims, we begin to glimpse some possibilities previously obscured: in particular, that the condition of the would-be desperationist might also be *addressed* — not merely *suppressed*.

Wild questions, then. What even more amazing but also perhaps more compelling acts might be undertaken by people who are currently willing to blow themselves up or fly airliners into skyscrapers for their cause? What if — just for one example — the absolute asceticism born of desperation took the form of unheard-of public acts of devotion, intended to shame us and also just as crucially to inspire?

Today's desperationists aim for a kind of *shattering* — of actual lives, places, symbols, and beyond these of our sense of predictability and reliability. It's not really "terror" strictly speaking.

But again, "shattering" is not something one answers with a declaration of war. The response it invites is more like an attempt to build in resiliency ... to weave systems together more flexibly ... making our lives more "shatter-proof." Let us seek ways to build cohesive and semi-self-sufficient neighborhoods in place of the diffuse collections of near-strangers so many of us now inhabit, with deeper bonds of co-reliance and mutual loyalty. *That's* real "security"!

What's the opposite of a fundamentalist? "Non-Religious" won't do. Many people are religious in non-fundamentalist ways; and anyway the non-religious do not want to be defined merely as lacking something the religious have. "Atheist" has the same problem: it's a good description of a few people (the Madalyn O'Hair type) who do define themselves by what they reject, but for most of the so-called non-religious the real point is that traditional religion, either its presence or its lack, just does not define our basic values or outlooks.

"Secular Humanist" then? But that phrase has been thoroughly corrupted by concerted rhetorical misconstruction. Moreover, many non-fundamentalists are neither secular nor humanist. Another problem is that "Humanism" itself is questionable for many of us who may actually be non-religious but who want to include the natural world within the sphere of deep value and concern.

We need a new term, something inspiring and substantive, not a mere negation of someone else's ultimate concern; also open-ended and clearly a big umbrella. I propose that we call ourselves **Spiritual Creatives.** "Spiritual" because we are in search of ultimate meaning and a deeper relation to each other and to nature, just not necessarily along established lines. "Creative" because unlike the literalists and traditionalists we recognize — and celebrate — our own role in giving shape to that spirituality. For the use of the term "creative" as a noun applicable to persons, I draw upon Paul Ray and Sherry Anderson's work identifying a third group beyond Traditionalism's rigidity and Modernism's economic and scientific convention-alism — "Cultural Creatives," fifty million strong in the USA today.[9]

The term **Spiritual Creatives** hints in turn that we might free up the language of "Creation" and even "Creationism" from the petrified grip of the reactionaries. Less than a quarter of the US public admits to believing in evolution — a bizarre little fact that ought to inspire a lot of thinking, not just dismissal and derision. What is it that so many people believe, or maybe even know, that evolution seems to offend?

Suppose we view evolution as the story of the self-generative creativity of life itself. Species respond, after all, to life's challenges and oppor-tunities — not consciously, not necessarily even purposefully, but surely in a way that we can describe as "intelligent" in an exact Websterian sense: "hav-ing the power of meeting a situation, especially a novel situation, by successful adjustment ..." We could call this **Evolutionary Creativity.** We could even argue that evolutionary creativity is exactly what contemporary so-called Creationism obscures and denies. A pesticide or antibiotic that kills 99% of the offending insects or bacteria will still leave a few to reproduce — variation within species will see to that — and soon enough we have a totally resistant population. This is why we are losing a higher percentage of crops to insects than before the widespread use of pesticides and why effective antibiotics are becoming ever more specialized and expensive and ever more temporarily effective. The world itself is intelligently creative!

20

Ally everywhere

Look for commonalities and common ground.
Build alliances from the areas of overlap
·rather than divergence. Make common cause as
much as possible. Speak to underlying interests
as much as to official positions, remembering
that interests themselves are fluid and complex.

We expect to take sides — and expect that
for each issue there will really be only two
sides to take. Each side is simple and uncompro-
mising. And yet, surely, when we consider things
carefully and are not in the heat of battle, we
know that the world is not like that at all. For
every issue, there are multiple sides, not just two;
each of them is itself complex and uncertain even

on key points and they overlap in unexpected and suggestive ways. The gay marriage debate, for example: how different it looks when you start by recognizing that the issue only arises in the first place because many gay couples *affirm* a central "traditional value" — marriage itself. Right away the whole issue shows up in a very different key.

Another approach to conflict is possible. The same battle-scarred and all-too-familiar landscapes can be viewed in very different and more creatively empowering way — the way of *common cause*.

Life *versus* Choice? But Life and Choice do not exclude each other. In fact, surely, we value as much as possible of both. We constantly have to balance them in every other area of life: think seat belt or speeding laws, food and pharmaceutical regulations, even decisions to go to war. Why not here? A sensible common agenda (let me say that again just to savor it: *a sensible common agenda*) would be to try to minimize their conflicts in real life. The question is not which value trumps which — but how we can keep them from coming into conflict in the first place.

Patriotism, the flag and "supporting the troops" always get lined up together, and on the "other" side. We know that the link must be broken. Part of our outrage, in fact, is how cynically our soldiers' honor and their very lives have been misused in the name of flag and country. But we haven't yet imagined what common cause with the troops would actually look like. We need a whole vision.

We tend to think that we're supporting the troops simply by opposing the war. But supporting the troops must *also* mean securing decent pay, medical care and education benefits back home. It means building and sustaining a society in which would-be soldiers have other decent choices, so that a "volunteer" really is a volunteer. It means making very sure that armed forces are sent on only the most necessary missions, collectively and openly debated. And it means rethinking their mission itself in a changing world. We need to argue for training peacekeepers as peacekeepers — a very different kind of training! — since that's a major part of what the troops are actually being sent to do.

In the end it isn't just "the troops," either. The interests underlying war fervor are often local jobs and regional prosperity. But local and regional interests would surely prefer, really, to keep young people working productively right in the area than risk their lives half a world away. Remember section 2: what if, instead of base closures and plant shut-downs, we could look forward to economic

conversion to help meet our massive infrastruc-
tural needs, such as solar energy facilities or new
kinds of farms?

Another tired polarization: fundamentalists versus "liberals." No possible allies here? But Martin
Luther King was a "fundamentalist" — only his
dream was rapture of a sort right here on Earth.
There are even environmentalist fundamentalists
and gay evangelicals, not to mention Jesus himself, that Jewish revolutionary who consorted with
prostitutes, apostates and the poorest of the poor.
"What would Jesus do?" the slogan asks. We too
often treat it lightly — "What would Jesus drive?"
"Who would Jesus bomb?" And sure, sometimes
the question is an occasion for people to project
their own moral prejudices onto God and then
read them back out as moral law. But the question
may also be asked in innocence and good faith.
There is much more potential here, a challenge
much more dramatic and unsettling. Just remember what Jesus *did* do: confront money-lenders in
the Temple, speak truth to power ...

Right-wing fundamentalists don't want Wal-
Mart destroying their communities or global
"entertainment" corporations colonizing their
children's imaginations any more than you or I
do. The back-to-earth, natural foods and natural

childbirth movements all have strong fundamentalist contingents. Pastors are beginning to speak of global warming with the alarm and passion until now reserved for gay marriage and *Roe v. Wade*. Alliances are there to be made.

21

The Tao of change

The wisdom of the martial arts: don't resist the
onrushing energy of opposition, but let it rush by,
use what you can, and as for the rest, work
cheerfully just beyond its reach.

Nothing is softer
or more yielding
than water.
Yet, given time,
it can erode even the hardest stone. That's
how the weak
can defeat the strong,
and the supple
can win out over the stiff.

Everybody knows it. So why don't we apply it
to our own lives?

— Tao Te Ching[10]

In opposition — when there really is opposition — we are tempted to meet force directly with force. No yielding! But the martial arts teach another approach. Yield by all means, sidestep the great energy of opposition, but as it rushes by, watch for ways in which the slightest nudge here or there might redirect things. Don't use your energy to oppose their energy. *Add* it to theirs instead, for the sake of changing direction.

The good old Stars and Stripes carries an immense load of emotion and identification, but when push comes to shove, the Left is ambivalent about even flying it, while the Right grabs it and runs every time. More of us were willing to show the flag right after 9/11, but even then reluctantly, knowing how readily it can be co-opted by right-wing and militaristic agendas — as it was.

This is a solvable problem. The flag is identi-fied with one particular kind of Americanism only because we have acquiesced. Let us reclaim the flag for the rest: for the free press and the balance of powers and the purple mountain majesties and diversity and tolerance and social self-reinvention. The next time the right grabs the flag and runs, how about running right along with them? In fact, grab the flag first. Let us plaster it not only all over our windmills and hybrid cars but over everything: every pro-multilateralist (i.e., what we used to call "anti-war") demonstration, every copy of the Bill of Rights the ACLU hands out in the street, our cars, our houses. Of course our vision of America differs — in some ways — from some of our fellow Americans'. That's to be expected in a diverse land. We affirm our commonality, still, by embracing the flag. We affirm our shared ideals. And of course if other people want to distinguish themselves from us, *they* can always march under some other banner, can't they?

Legal gay marriage may be a while. We can retreat into bitterness or continue to batter away at the familiar obstacles — and that's vital work. But there are also other and entirely differently inventive ways to work cheerfully just beyond opposition's reach. Such as: let us invent a new form of committed relationship. Let us make it *better than marriage* — or really wonderful in some other directions: more celebratory, more creatively articulated, more communal (meaning, maybe, that the support and conviviality of others is built in from the start). As sacred as you like, too: maybe a good label would be "Covenant" — something evocative but clearly new. Meanwhile, separately, establish a relatively standardized list of choices for civil unions or other kinds of contractual conjoinings of resources or interests (because no law under capitalism is going to ban *contracts*, is it?). Sympathetic spiritual assemblies can just start performing such Covenants, and of course not only for same-sex couples but for anyone who wants the benefits of Better-Than-Marriage. In France, it turns out, most takers for civil contracts are straight.

I know, I know, traditional marriage will continue to be favored in law and policy. All the more reason to make Better-Than-Marriage *really good*. And you think the Right will simply appropriate the good stuff? Really? From gay people? And if they do — wonderful! Make a free, vocal, visible gift. Even some conservatives now argue for entirely splitting civil marriage from religious marriage. Different denominations could do as they please, and the role of the state is simply to guarantee contracts. Fine. Hurrah for conservatism! Fundamentalists, meanwhile, are promoting more restrictive kinds of marriage. Apparently they too think that marriage can be improved...

22

Do it now

Look for ways to make change right now, on your own or with readily-present like-minded others. Do it yourself! Why not right now? Why not right here?

New kinds of communities, new governments, new types of art, new ways to live — a great many changes, even radical changes, can be made right now. They do not need permission or consensus. Why wait? Despite our usual imaginative inertia, despite the social forwardness of just going and "doing something," real change is often already well within our powers.

In 2006 Wisconsin citizens' groups organized a People's Legislature — a delegate assembly openly elected by anyone who chose to take part, except without campaign advertising and the other usual distortions. Would-be voters had to show up and actually discuss the issues. The assembly in turn launched right into the issues that the official Legislature, beholden to lobbyists and entrenched political interests right and left, will not touch.

Tired of inept or evasive local governments? People have simply organized their own, circulating petitions proposing new neighborhood representatives and offering themselves as candidates while also inviting others. Duties are proposed: keeping people informed, organizing forums and support groups, liaison with other elected officials.

What is this? People actually *creating new governments* alongside the problematic or incomplete structures already in place? This is what democracy looks like!

Oh, and while we're at it: could anything of the sort be done on a *global* scale? Do-it-yourself world government? Section 5 proposed using person-to-person virtual contact to build ongoing worldwide political organizations based on direct contact between people, and even making a whole new representative structure out of "virtual districts." You or I or anyone could make a start, right now, today.

We might also notice that many of the necessary connections actually already exist, only they
are not framed politically — yet. Bill Mollison
proposes a new kind of United Nations in which a
"nation" is defined by a shared ethic and culture,
where all those sharing an "ethic of earth care"
might therefore come together (he notes for
example that there are far fewer active members
of political parties than there are organic gardeners) to "share resources in a humane alliance."

> Global seed exchanges, gardening forums
> and regional groups already meet and are
> increasing in cooperation. There are already
> alternative economic summits, bioregional
> congresses, tribal conferences, garden and
> farm design groups. What remains is to
> unify them, to meet together, to count
> numbers and to recognize each other's
> rights. A concept of a global nation is, in
> fact, very well developed in such groups.[11]

Try this one: do-it-yourself money. Today's
money system increasingly enables wealth to be
pulled out of any region of a country and massively
concentrated and redirected with absolutely no
responsiveness to local communities and people.
This kind of wealth-extraction is becoming both

more intense and more visible as corporate reach goes global — but at the same time it may seem that nothing short of global financial revolution could stop it. Money is money is money.

But even money can change — and *is* changing. Initiatives all over North America are creating local currencies: forms of money that are simply not exchangeable beyond the community. These currencies automatically keep money in the area, support local producers and encourage use and re-use of local rather than distant resources. They build face-to-face community. My local alternative money — "NC Plenty" — highlights local scenes and animals on the bills: spreading oaks, old mills, herons and other water creatures from this region of textile producers and slow-running rivers. Look around: I bet your area has one too. If not ...

23

Go for broke

Imagine not just two steps down the road, but all
the way. Take your vision and multiply it by itself.
What unheard-of possibilities lie all around us,
right here and right now?

Never let it be said that you erred on the side
of caution. Aim way too high. See where
sheer imaginative chutzpah can go. Get so wild
that even the idealists look timid.

After leading some workshops at Lakehead
University in Thunder Bay, Ontario, I am in a
nearby wilderness with my host and friend Bob
Jickling for a weekend retreat with some colleagues
and students. It's January; snow is everywhere,
lightly filtering down from the trees in the sunlight.

Our days are spent skiing and snowshoeing in the shadow of a large connected set of mesas that ends and anchors the long peninsula, jutting out into Lake Superior, which forms the "bay" of Thunder Bay. Sleeping Giant it is called, which is just how it looks in silhouette.

Evenings around the cabin fire, we retell stories. First Nations people say that Sleeping Giant is an enstoned brave, punished for revealing the silver deposit that once drew miners to the islets just offshore. Or possibly a protective figure. The legends also speak of the Giant awakening, rising again, to protect land and lake. From the students and Thunder Bay natives we hear how captivating is the Giant on a daily basis, the figure across the bay always a presence in their lives. People choose their dwellings to be sure to have a daily view. They speak of leaving and returning, the first glimpse of the Giant after a stint away, how it draws them back.

Late on the last night, heavy snow falling, a dear friend reads aloud from a collection of Gary Snyder's early writings. Snyder's young, bumming around Yosemite:

> Sitting on a boulder at El Capitan beach
> — water, soft green willow, young girls

swimming — silver-green pines, and above
it all the cliff.

A brown bear and two cubs. Smell of
mint. Pine needles in the light dust. Athens
and Rome, Good-bye![12]

Up before the sun the next day, shoveling our
way out to the car, we can see the Giant come to life
— perhaps that is part of the truth of the story,
that it comes to life again every morning? — its new
snow shimmering in the purple and orange sunrise
long before the sun reaches our lakeside cabin. I
am reminded of Uluru, the iconic rock formation
of Central Australia, land of the Aboriginals, likewise blazing a brilliant red at sunrise and sunset
while the surrounding flatland lies in darkness.

Driving back, Bob and I mull over that line:
"Athens and Rome, Good-bye!" Will our century
see truly new world centers emerge? Beijing,
Brasilia? But what comes into view need not be
simply a realignment of existing centers of power.
The new centers could be — maybe *must* be —
places of emergence of something fresh, something bigger: a reinvention of the city, of human
possibility itself. Places where the powers of larger-
than-human worlds and human worlds newly meet,
cross-fertilize, synergize.

Then the last piece falls into place. After Athens and Rome, why not Thunder Bay? This very place! Not the city alone, I mean, but the bay itself, the city *and* the Giant. Why not? Really, why not? It's not a matter of size: in human terms Thunder Bay is already larger than Athens or Rome in their heydays. It's rather that this place has the stories, the magic, the more-than-human presence — another morning of the world.

In fact, why don't we ask the question of all the places we inhabit or even just visit? What if *this* place — any place, every place — were to be the new Athens or Rome? What kind of civilization could arise *here*? What unheard-of gifts could be offered to the future by your very own place? And — by *you*?

Afterword

A deep bow of thanks, first of all, to my fellow travelers in the adventures that led up to this book and that I am sure will lead beyond: especially to Bolton Anthony, Jim Cheney, Meredith Emmett, Sally Goerner, Patsy Hallen, Bob Jickling, Mike Neeley, Beth Raps, John Sullivan, to my family ... and to so many others. Blessings to you all.

Helpful works on creative methods, though in much more everyday keys, are Edward DeBono's *Serious Creativity* (HarperCollins, 1992) and *Lateral Thinking* (Harper, 1970); and Barry Nalebuff and Ian Ayres, *Why Not? How to Use Everyday Ingenuity to Solve Problems Big and Small* (Harvard Business School Press, 2003). On proactive thinking, Stephen Covey's *Seven Habits of Highly Effective People* (Simon & Schuster, 1990) is a classic. Two other books of my own are *Creativity for Critical Thinkers* and *Creative Problem-Solving in Ethics,* both from Oxford University Press, 2007. Specific methods for organizing creative thinking in groups include the World Café (Juanita Brown, *The World Café,* Berrett-Koehler, 2005, or theworldcafe.com), Open Space Forum (Harrison Owen, *Open Space Technology: A User's Guide,* Berrett-Koehler, 1997), and Appreciative Inquiry (appreciativeinquiry.case.edu).

On all of this book's specific themes there are multitudinous websites. Indeed there were times writing this book when it seemed like I or my students could barely dream up anything without someone letting me know, a day or so later, that it was already happening somewhere, and sending me a link. All manner of sustainability projects and local currencies; various forms of "delightism" (for just one, check out improveverywhere.com); alternatives to marriage (unmarried.org) and to war, travel, work, oil (i4at.org); people who are putting cutting-edge technologies to immediate and inventive good use everywhere, like jerry-rigging 200-mpg plug-in hybrids or documenting voting irregularities and posting the videos online (videothevote.org).

You see the problem, though: get started on all this and quickly it's another book. An intriguing snapshot of imaginative innovation right now, I am sure, but not so usable as a prospective handbook for the imagination. So despite continuing temptation, I refrain from citing specific sites.

In any case creative juxtaposition is better served by you mostly finding your own way into what's happening. Here are just two starting points (if you wish):

worldchanging.com

globalideasbank.org

Further reading? I have the same caveat: there is a *vast* literature, and mostly it's best if you find your own ways into it. For just a small shelf of books to get started, my suggestions are:

Christopher Alexander. *A Pattern Language.* Oxford, 1977. "Timeless" ways of building, on all scales.

David Bornstein. *How to Change the World: Social Entrepreneurs and the Power of New Ideas.* Oxford, 2004.

Stewart Brand. *The Clock of the Long Now.* Basic, 1999. Projects to "radically lengthen cultural memory."

Malcolm Gladwell. *The Tipping Point.* Little, Brown, 2000. "How little things can make a big difference."

Sally Goerner. *After the Clockwork Universe: The Emerging Science and Culture of Integral Society.* Floris Books, 1999.

Paul Goodman. *Utopian Essays and Practical Proposals*. Vintage, 1962.

Paul Hawken, Hunter and Amory Lovins. *Natural Capitalism*. Little, Brown, 1999.

Ivan Illich. *Tools for Conviviality*. Perennial Library, 1973.

Herbert Marcuse. *One-Dimensional Man*. Beacon, 1964.

Frederick Turner. *The New World*. Princeton University Press, 1985.

One other book of mine, *Back to Earth: Tomorrow's Environmentalism* (Temple University Press, 1994).

And two journals: *Utne Reader* at utne.com and *Yes: A Journal of Positive Futures* yesmagazine.org.

Good luck!

Notes

1. Juliet Schor. *The Overworked American.* Basic Books, 1992, p. 2.
2. Gregory Lamb. "How to go to MIT for free." *Christian Science Monitor,* January 1, 2007, pp. 13-14.
3. Rob Brezsny. *Pronoia Is the Antidote for Paranoia: How the Whole World Is Conspiring to Shower You with Blessings.* North Atlantic, 2005, p. 32.
4. Bill Mollison. *Permaculture: A Designer's Manual.* Tagari, 1988, p. 15.
5. Bo Lozoff. "Getting Free." Interview with Derrick Jensen in *The Sun,* December 2000, p. 21.
6. Schor, p. 133.
7. Bruce Wilshire. *Wild Hunger: The Primal Roots of Modern Addiction.* Rowman & Littlefield, 1999, Chapter 1.
8. Richard Louv. *Last Child in the Woods: Saving our Children from Nature-Deficit Disorder.* Algonquin, 2006.
9. Paul Ray and Sherry Anderson. *The Cultural Creatives: How 50 Million People are Changing the World.* Three Rivers Press, 2000.
10. Opening of section 78 of the *Tao Te Ching,* interpreted here by Ron Hogan and available at beatrice.com/TAO.
11. Mollison, p. 508.
12. Gary Snyder and Tom Killion. *The High Sierra of California.* Heyday Books, 2002, p. 66.

If you have enjoyed *How To Re-imagine the World*
you might also enjoy other

BOOKS TO BUILD A NEW SOCIETY

Our books provide positive solutions for people
who want to make a difference. We specialize in:

Environment and Justice • Conscientious Commerce • Sustainable Living
Ecological Design and Planning • Natural Building & Appropriate Technology
New Forestry • Educational and Parenting Resources • Nonviolence
Progressive Leadership • Resistance and Community

New Society Publishers

ENVIRONMENTAL BENEFITS STATEMENT

New Society Publishers has chosen to produce this book on recycled paper
made with **100% post consumer waste**, processed chlorine free, and old
growth free.

For every 5,000 books printed, New Society saves the following resources:[1]

9	Trees
832	Pounds of Solid Waste
915	Gallons of Water
1,193	Kilowatt Hours of Electricity
1,512	Pounds of Greenhouse Gases
7	Pounds of HAPs, VOCs, and AOX Combined
2	Cubic Yards of Landfill Space

[1]Environmental benefits are calculated based on research done by the
Environmental Defense Fund and other members of the Paper Task Force who
study the environmental impacts of the paper industry.

For a full list of NSP's titles, please call 1-800-567-6772 or check out our website at:

www.newsociety.com

NEW SOCIETY PUBLISHERS